Growing Up with AI

Artificial Intelligence for everyday Use

Amaara Verma & Abeer Verma

Fusion Books

Publisher	:	**Fusion Books** X-30, Okhla Industrial Area, Phase-II New Delhi-110020
Phone	:	011- 40712200
E-mail	:	wecare@diamondbooks.in
Website	:	www.diamondbooks.in
Edition	:	2026

AUTHOR'S NOTE

Growing up today means growing up with Artificial Intelligence.
For Abeer, AI first felt exciting — like unlocking hidden features inside everyday apps.
For Amaara, it felt bigger — not just about tools, but about how AI shapes habits, friendships, creativity, and even identity.

We realized something important:
AI isn't just a subject.
It's an environment.
It influences the music we hear, the content we scroll, the way we study, and the way we express ourselves.

This book is not about coding complex algorithms.
It's about understanding how AI quietly shapes your everyday life — your studies, routines, emotions, communication, and future.

If you have ever wondered:
- Should I use AI for homework?
- Is AI changing how we think?
- How do I stay safe online?
- Will AI affect my future career?
- Can I use AI creatively without losing my originality?

Then this book is for you.
You are not competing with AI.
You are growing alongside it.
And how you grow matters.

— Abeer & Amaara

Preface – Why This Book Matters

We are the first generation in history to grow up surrounded by intelligent systems.

Artificial Intelligence is not something "coming soon."
It is already embedded in classrooms, social media, search engines, shopping apps, fitness trackers, and entertainment platforms.
But access is not the same as awareness.

Growing Up with AI is designed to help students:
- Understand what AI actually is
- Recognize where it operates in daily life
- Use AI tools thoughtfully and productively
- Think critically about bias, privacy, and misinformation
- Prepare for a future shaped by intelligent systems

This book blends two essential perspectives:
Abeer's focus on how AI tools function and how to use them effectively.
Amaara's focus on reflection — asking what AI means for identity, society, and ethical decision-making.

Together, they create a balanced guide for the modern teen.
AI will not define your future.
Your awareness will.

FOREWORD

Artificial Intelligence has moved from laboratories into living rooms and classrooms.
Unlike previous technological revolutions, AI does not merely assist — it influences decision-making, personalization, and even perception.

For young people, this presents both opportunity and responsibility. What makes Growing Up with AI distinctive is that it is written from within the generation it addresses. Abeer Verma and Amaara Verma do not write as distant observers, but as participants in the AI-powered ecosystem.

Abeer brings clarity to the mechanics of AI tools and their practical use.
Amaara brings reflection to questions of ethics, identity, and digital culture.

Together, they offer not alarmism, but awareness.
Not hype, but balance.
In a world shaped by algorithms, informed students become empowered citizens.

This book encourages young readers to grow not only technologically skilled, but intellectually independent and ethically grounded.

INDEX

Chapter 1

What Is AI, Really?

"Wait… Is That AI Too?"

Imagine this: You ask your phone, "What's the capital of Japan?" and it instantly replies, "Tokyo."
You open Instagram, and your feed magically shows reels about football, fashion, or funny cats—exactly what you love.
Later, a smart app reminds you to drink water, and your playlist recommends new music that somehow feels perfect for your mood.

Guess what?
That's AI working quietly in the background.
But what exactly is AI? Is it a robot? A software? Magic?
Let's break it down.

What Is Artificial Intelligence (AI)?

At its simplest, Artificial Intelligence is the ability of machines (like your phone, apps, or websites) to “think,” “learn,” and “act” like humans—but through data and algorithms.

It’s not human, but it mimics human-like tasks:
• Understanding your voice
• Recognizing patterns (like your taste in memes)
• Making suggestions (like next steps or songs)
• Solving problems (like map directions)

AI = Smart Software that Learns from Data

Real-Life Example: AI in Your Pocket

Think about these everyday tools:
• **Google Assistant / Siri / Alexa** – They understand your voice, answer your questions, and even tell jokes!
• **Netflix & YouTube** – They recommend shows you might like based on your past watching habits.
• **Grammarly or ChatGPT** – They help you write better, correct grammar, and even generate ideas.

You don’t need to be a tech geek or coder to use AI. If you’re reading this on a phone or laptop—you’re already part of the AI world.

How Does AI Actually Work?

Imagine you’re teaching a robot to recognize a dog. You show it 1000 images of dogs and say, “These are dogs.”
The robot looks at fur, ears, tail, nose… and learns. Now, even if you show it a new dog picture, it says: “Hey, this looks like a dog!”
This is called machine learning, a branch of AI where computers learn from data and examples, just like we do.

AI uses:
• **Data** (lots of it!)

- **Algorithms** (rules and steps)
- **Feedback loops** (to improve over time)

School-Life AI: It's Already Here!

Let's look at how AI quietly helps you as a student:

School Task	How AI Helps
Homework Help	Chatbots like ChatGPT or Google Gemini explain difficult concepts
Revision	Quizlet or AI-based flashcards help you test yourself
Essay Writing	Grammarly or ProWritingAid helps fix grammar and flow
Research	Perplexity AI gives quick summaries of websites or topics

Notes Notion AI summarizes lectures or textbooks in simple form
It's like having a digital study buddy available 24/7!

Types of AI You Should Know

Let's keep this simple. There are 3 levels of AI you'll hear about:
1. Narrow AI (or Weak AI):
This is the AI we use every day—good at specific tasks.

Examples: Google Translate, ChatGPT, Netflix recommendations.

2. General AI (not here yet):
This AI would be able to think and reason like a human. It's still under research.

3. Super AI (sci-fi stuff!):
An AI smarter than humans in every way. Think of Iron Man's

JARVIS. Cool, but not real (yet!).

For now, Narrow AI is what we live with—and it's more powerful than you think.

Common Myths About AI (Busted!)

Myth 1: AI is only for coders and computer geeks.
✓ **Fact:** AI is for everyone—students, artists, athletes, even writers like you!

Myth 2: AI will take over all jobs.
✓ **Fact:** AI will change jobs, but not all will disappear. In fact, new AI-powered jobs are being created every day.

Myth 3: AI is 100% accurate and unbiased.
✓ **Fact:** AI can make mistakes or show bias—it learns from human data, which can be flawed. That's why human judgment is still important.

Teen Talk: So, Why Should You Care?

Here's why every teen should understand AI:

- **It's everywhere** – Whether you like it or not, AI is part of your world.
- **It saves time** – Helps in studying, planning, and organizing.
- **It makes you smarter** – You can get answers faster, but only if you ask the right questions.
- **It boosts creativity** – Want to create a song, poster, or comic? AI tools can help you start.

Knowing how to use AI wisely = having a superpower in your pocket.

Fun Tools to Explore (Right Now!)

Try these AI-powered tools:

- **ChatGPT** (chat.openai.com) – Ask questions, get explanations.
- **Grammarly** (grammarly.com) – Fix grammar and clarity.
- **Notion AI** (notion.so/ai) – Smart note-taking.
- **Canva Magic** (canva.com) – Create art or presentations.
- **Suno (suno.ai)** – Make your own music!

Don't worry about "knowing everything." Just start exploring, and learn as you go.

Try This: Quick AI Scavenger Hunt

✓ Open your phone. List 3 apps that use AI.
✓ Use an AI chatbot to summarize today's news in 3 lines.
✓ Ask ChatGPT to explain a difficult school topic in rap form.
✓ Use Canva's AI tools to design a poster about "Smart Study Habits."
Now reflect: How did these tools help? What felt easy? What felt "too much"?

Let's Reflect

- Have you ever used AI without realizing it?
- Do you think AI makes your day easier or more confusing?
- How can you balance using AI with thinking for yourself?

Abeer's Tech Tip
Try tracking how many times you interact with AI in one day — search engines, recommendations, filters, voice assistants. Awareness is the first step to understanding.
Amaara Asks
If AI quietly influences what we see every day, how much of our thinking is truly independent?

Chapter Summary

- AI = Smart technology that learns from data and helps in tasks.
- You already use AI daily—in school apps, phones, music, and searches.
- AI works by recognizing patterns and improving through feedback.
- Teens can use AI to study better, save time, and express creativity.
- Being aware of AI gives you an edge in your daily life and future career.

Chapter 2

AI Agents All Around You

Smart Tools in Your Everyday Life

Welcome to Your AI-Home

Imagine this:
You wake up.
Your smart alarm plays soft music at just the right time.
Your smartwatch buzzes, showing your sleep score and heart rate.
In the kitchen, your smart fridge suggests breakfast recipes.
You check your phone—your calendar is already set, and your favorite playlist starts on its own.

All of this?
AI agents working silently behind the scenes.
They don't have faces or metal bodies like robots in movies.
But they're smart.
They learn your habits.
They help you live better.

What Is an AI Agent?

An AI agent is a program or system that:
- **Senses** (takes in information)
- **Thinks** (analyzes what's needed)
- **Acts** (gives a result or takes action)

Think of them as mini digital assistants that make decisions based on data.
And guess what?
You already live with dozens of them—on your phone, in your apps, in your browser, even in your home!

Where Are These Agents Hiding?

Let's look at some everyday areas where AI agents help:

1. Phones & Smart Devices
- Google Assistant, Siri, Alexa – Voice-based AI agents that set alarms, give directions, or answer trivia.
- Face Unlock or Fingerprint Scanners – Use AI to recognize you securely.
- Keyboard Predictive Text – Learns your typing style and predicts your next word.

2. Entertainment & Music
- Spotify, YouTube, Netflix Recommendations – AI agents learn your watching or listening habits and suggest new content.
- Reels & Shorts Algorithms – Instagram, TikTok, and YouTube AI decide which content to show you next.

3. Online Shopping
- Amazon Suggests What You'll Like – AI agents analyze what you search, click, and buy.

• Chatbots Help You Shop – AI-powered assistants help you return products, track orders, or choose items.

4. Study & School Life

• Grammarly, ChatGPT, Notion AI – Writing help, summaries, and organization tools.

• Smart Planners – Apps like Reclaim.ai schedule tasks automatically based on your availability.

5. Smart Home Gadgets

• Fridges that track groceries and expiry dates.

• Smart bulbs that adjust brightness based on time of day.

• Smart thermostats that learn when you're cold or warm.

Real-Life Teen Examples

Let's meet a few imaginary teens using AI agents every day:

Ananya (16, Class 11)

Uses Notion AI to auto-summarize her History notes.

Her Google Calendar is managed by Reclaim, which reschedules tasks if she misses one.

Spotify knows her study-time vibe = Lo-fi beats.

Rishi (15, Class 10)

Uses ChatGPT to practice English essays.

He checks Suno.ai to generate background music for his school play.

He uses Alexa to set water reminders.

Zoya (17, aspiring YouTuber)

Uses OpusClip to auto-edit her videos.

Canva Magic tool helps her create thumbnails.

Shortwave AI summarizes her overflowing Gmail inbox.

Why Are These Agents So "Smart"?

Because they learn from:
• Your inputs (what you type, say, or click)
• Your patterns (when and how often you do things)
• Your preferences (what you like or avoid)

They're not thinking like humans—but they are adapting to you. AI agents are like invisible helpers who get better the more you use them.

Quick List: AI Agents You Can Explore

Agent Name	What It Does	Where to Use It
ChatGPT	Chat, write, plan, code	Web & App
Google Gemini	Personal assistant	Android, Web
Reclaim.ai	Smart calendar	Desktop
Notion AI	Notes, study plans	Desktop/Mobile
Suno.ai	Music creation	Web
Canva Magic	Posters, visuals	Web/App
Alexa / Siri	Voice control	Smart devices
Motion / SkedPal	Schedule planning	Productivity apps

What About Privacy?

Yes, AI agents track data to help you better—but:
• You should check app permissions
• Use private mode when needed
• Be mindful of what you share

Never give personal passwords, locations, or personal photos to unknown bots or apps.

Try This: Spot the Agent!

Take a normal day and write down:

1. What time you wake up
2. What music you hear
3. Which app you use for school
4. What YouTube shows you watch
5. What appears on your shopping list

Now ask yourself—did AI suggest or assist in any of those?
Most likely: Yes! You're surrounded by AI agents.

Compare: Human Assistant vs. AI Agent

Task	Human Assistant	AI Agent
Remind you to drink water	May forget	Never forgets
Suggest new music	Based on own taste	Based on your taste
Plan your day	Needs your input	Can auto plan
Write essays	Gives ideas	Can generate drafts instantly
Talk back to you	Real emotion	Programmed responses

AI can be helpful, but it's not human. Use both wisely!

Tips to Make the Most of AI Agents

- **Explore Settings** – Many apps have hidden AI features (like auto-scheduling, smart replies).
- **Don't Over-Rely** – Use AI to assist, not replace your thinking.
- **Stay Updated** – New AI tools launch every month. Try one new tool each week.

• **Practice Safe Sharing** – AI agents don't forget, so be careful with private data.

Let's Reflect

• Which AI agent do you use the most?
• Did you ever use AI without realizing it?
• How would your day change without AI tools?

Chapter Summary

• AI agents are smart programs that act on your behalf using data and learning.
• They exist in your phones, apps, browsers, smartwatches, fridges—even classrooms!
• From reminders to entertainment, study tools to planners, these agents boost your daily life.
• Know how they work, what data they collect, and how to use them responsibly.

Chapter 3

Using AI to Study Smarter

Notes, Summaries, Quizzes & More

"Wish Studying Felt Easier?"

Have you ever stared at a long history chapter and thought:
"I wish someone could just explain this in simple terms..."
Or felt like your brain is full but your revision isn't done?
Or you wanted flashcards but had no time to make them?
Welcome to the world of AI-powered study tools—where apps help you learn, summarize faster, quiz smarter, and remember more, without burning out.
AI isn't just for techies—it's your secret study partner.

Why Use AI for Studying?

Because smart students today don't study harder—they study smarter.
AI helps you:
• Save time while revising

- Understand tough topics in easier ways
- Get instant feedback on essays or grammar
- Stay organized with planning tools
- Generate quizzes or flashcards in one click

Imagine having a personal tutor that works 24/7—AI makes that possible.

Real Teen Life: Meet Shreya

Shreya, a 16-year-old science student, had 5 chapters to revise in 2 days.

Here's how she used AI:

- ChatGPT to explain "Photosynthesis" in her own words
- Notion AI to summarize textbook pages into bullet points
- Quizlet AI to generate flashcards from her notes
- Grammarly to polish her English essay
- Reclaim.ai to auto-block time slots in her calendar

In 3 hours, she got more done than a full day of "just reading."
That's the power of AI + smart studying.

AI Tools You Can Use for Studying

Here are top AI tools that can help you master schoolwork:

Tool	What It Does	Link
ChatGPT	Explains, rewrites, answers questions	chat.openai.com
Perplexity AI	Homework search with sources	perplexity.ai
Notion AI	Summarizes long notes, auto-organizes	notion.so/ai
Quizlet AI	Flashcards, MCQs, quizzes	quizlet.com

Grammarly AI	Writing feedback	grammarly.com
PDFgear AI	Read + summarize PDF books	pdfgear.com
Microsoft Copilot	In-built AI in MS Word/Excel	microsoft.com

How to Use These in Your Routine

1. Understand Tough Topics with ChatGPT

- **Ask:** "Explain Newton's laws in simple words."
- **Or:** "Summarize Mughal history in bullet points."
- **Try:** "Write a 100-word summary of Macbeth for Class 10."

Tip: Always double-check facts with textbooks. AI gives quick help but isn't your final source.

2. Make Smart Notes with Notion AI

- Paste your long notes. Click "Summarize."
- **Want mind maps? Ask:** "Convert this to bullet points + add headings."
- Create revision checklists.

Bonus: You can even share these notes with friends!

3. Auto-Create Flashcards with Quizlet

- Paste a paragraph or topic. AI makes flashcards instantly.
- Practice in different modes: Learn, Write, Spell, Test.

Fast, fun, and perfect for last-minute revision.

4. Fix Essays & Grammar with Grammarly

- Paste your assignment.
- **It checks:**
    - o Grammar
    - o Tone
    - o Clarity
    - o Vocabulary

• Makes your writing look sharp—even for school competitions or emails!

5. Study PDFs the Smart Way

Using PDFgear AI, you can:
• Summarize long chapters
• Extract key points
• Ask questions from the text
Works great for NCERT PDFs, reference books, and research.

6. Plan Your Study Time with AI Calendars

Tools like:
• Reclaim.ai
• Motion
• SkedPal

Can:
• Detect your free time
• Schedule study blocks
• Remind you to take breaks!
Your brain needs focus and rest—AI helps you balance both.

Try This: Smart Study Day Challenge

Pick your next study session and do this:

Task	AI Tool
Understand chapter	ChatGPT
Summarize notes	Notion AI
Create flashcards	Quizlet
Fix grammar	Grammarly
Plan time	Reclaim

At the end of the session, ask:
"Did I learn faster? Did I feel less tired?"

Most students say yes!

Balance: AI Helps, But Don't Let It Think For You

Here's a golden rule:
Let AI assist your brain, not replace it.

Use AI for:
✓ Understanding difficult ideas
✓ Organizing better
✓ Practicing smarter

Don't use AI for:
× Copy-pasting entire homework
× Avoiding real learning
× Cheating on assignments
Remember, learning is a muscle. AI is a tool. You still need to think.

Let's Reflect

- Have you used any AI tool to study before?
- What do you find hardest about studying—and can AI help?
- How can you create a healthy balance between tech and thinking?

Case Study: AI in CBSE Schools

Did you know some CBSE schools now use:
- AI-powered digital boards
- Adaptive learning apps
- Student dashboards for tracking progress

Teachers are learning AI tools too. The goal is not just to teach about AI, but to help use AI for better learning outcomes.

You're part of a new generation of AI-empowered learners.

Talk With Your Friends

Start a "Study with AI" group.

Share tips, tools, and best ways to:
- Remember better
- Learn faster
- Stay motivated

Learning is more fun together—even when it's with robots!

Abeer's Tech Tip
Use AI to generate practice questions instead of answers. It strengthens learning more than simply copying solutions.
Amaara Asks
If AI helps us finish faster, are we learning deeper — or just becoming more efficient?

Chapter Summary

- AI helps you study smarter—not harder.
- You can use tools like ChatGPT, Notion AI, Grammarly, and Quizlet for notes, summaries, writing, and revision.
- These tools save time, make learning fun, and build confidence.
- Don't misuse AI—use it to support your learning, not replace your effort.

Chapter 4

AI for Communication & Social Life

Write, Chat, Post & Connect Smarter

"Talk Smarter, Post Better"

You're about to send a message to your teacher.
You pause.

You don't want to sound too casual… or too robotic.
You're replying to a DM on Instagram and want to add something witty.
Or you're writing a caption for a reel and feel stuck.

Here's the good news:
AI can help you talk, write, post, and express yourself better—while saving time and sounding like YOU.

Let's explore how.

What Is AI in Communication?

AI in communication means using smart tools to:

- Write better
- Translate faster
- Check tone
- Reply instantly
- Craft social media content
- Even hold conversations!

Whether it's for school emails or Snapchat replies, AI makes communication clearer, faster, and smarter.

Where Teens Use AI to Communicate Daily

You might not realize it, but these AI-powered actions happen every day:

Task	AI Behind It
Auto-correcting typos	Smart keyboard (Gboard, SwiftKey)
Email reply suggestions	Gmail Smart Reply
Caption suggestions	Instagram Reels AI
Language translation	Google Translate
Voice typing	AI speech recognition
Chat with bots	Customer service, mental health apps
Comment moderation	AI filters on social apps

You don't need to be fluent in English or a grammar expert—AI gives you communication superpowers.

Writing Help Tools: From Awkward to Awesome

Tools You'll Love:

Tool	What It Helps With
Grammarly AI	Grammar, tone, clarity, vocabulary
ChatGPT	Draft messages, emails, bios
Writesonic / Copy.ai	Instagram captions, tweets, ad copy
Quillbot	Rewording & paraphrasing
Hemingway Editor	Makes writing bold & clear
Canva Magic Write	Generate social media posts

Try This:
Ask ChatGPT:
"Write a birthday message for my best friend that's funny and heart-felt."

Emailing Like a Pro (With AI Help)

Let's say you're emailing your teacher:
Bad:
"Ma'am I won't be coming. Please adjust."

Better (AI-polished):
"Dear Ma'am, I hope you are well. I won't be able to attend class today due to a personal reason. Kindly consider my absence. Thank you."
✓ AI helps check grammar, correct tone, and make you sound respectful and professional.

Top AI Tip:
Use Gmail's "Smart Compose" and "Smart Reply" features—they write part of the message for you!

Instagram, Reels & Captions – AI Style

Let's face it—writing a perfect caption can take longer than recording the reel!

AI tools like:
• Copy.ai
• ChatGPT
• Canva Magic

can generate:
• Reel captions
• Hashtags
• Post descriptions
• Comment responses
• Bio ideas

Example Prompt:
"Write a cool caption for my reel on school life + funny twist."

You can edit it later, but AI gives you a great start.

Talk to the World – Language Translation & Accessibility

Want to talk to someone in French? Hindi? Tamil? Spanish?

AI makes it easy.
• **Google Translate** – Translate text, voice, or photos instantly.
• **DeepL** – Professional-quality translations.
• **Voice Translator AI** – Convert voice to text across languages.

Accessibility Bonus:
Many tools also help students with reading/writing challenges by using text-to-speech or speech-to-text AI.

Chatbots – More Than Just Talking Robots

You've probably used a chatbot on:
- A school website
- A shopping app
- A wellness page

These AI tools:
- Answer FAQs
- Help you navigate platforms
- Offer emotional support (like Wysa or Replika)
- Provide reminders and encouragement

Important: Chatbots are helpful—but they are not human friends. Use them wisely.

Mindful Communication – What AI Can't Do

While AI can write better texts, it can't:
- Understand sarcasm deeply
- Feel emotions
- Judge social context the way humans do

That's why you must always review AI-generated content.

Ask:
- Is it appropriate for this person?
- Does it sound like me?
- Could this message hurt someone?

Try This: AI + Communication Challenge

Over 1 day, try these:

Activity	Use AI To…
Email teacher	Fix grammar using Grammarly
Write post caption	Generate with Copy.ai
DM friend in Spanish	Use Google Translate
Fix your school project bio	Use ChatGPT to rewrite it
Respond to comments	Use Smart Reply or Canva

At the end, ask:
"Did AI help me say what I meant?"
"Did I feel more confident?"
"Did I still sound like me?"

AI & Social Media Manners

Be smart. Be safe. Be kind.

Here are golden rules:
1. Don't copy-paste AI replies blindly. Always personalize.
2. Don't ghost or spam using auto-replies. Stay human.
3. Don't use AI to fake identities, insult others, or post false information.
4. Use tone-checkers if you're unsure if your message sounds rude.

Remember, being kind is smarter than sounding smart.

Let's Reflect

- Have you ever said something wrong online and wished you had help?
- How can AI make your posts or replies better?

• Where should you not use AI to talk?

Pro Tip: Build Your "AI Style"

• Use AI to find your own communication tone:
– Funny?
– Smart?
– Motivational?

Start building a voice that people recognize as you—with AI as your coach, not your clone.

Chapter Summary

• AI helps you write, post, chat, and reply better across school, social media, and life.
• You can use tools like ChatGPT, Grammarly, Canva, and Translate to express clearly.
• Always review and personalize AI responses.
• Use AI to build confidence—not to copy others.

Chapter 5

Fitness, Food & Fun – The AI Way

Get Healthier, Happier, and Fitter with Smart Tools

"Can AI Help Me Feel Better?"

It's 7 a.m. Your smart alarm wakes you gently with birdsong.
Your smartwatch buzzes: "You slept for 6.5 hours. Time to hydrate!"
By 8 a.m., your breakfast is a bowl of oats—recommended by your health app.
By evening, you've done a 20-minute AI-guided workout, discovered a new lo-fi playlist, and tracked your steps.

Welcome to the AI-powered wellness lifestyle—designed just for you.

AI doesn't just help you study or write. It also helps you:

- Eat better
- Move more
- Sleep smarter

• Chill out
• And have fun

Let's explore how to use AI to upgrade your body, brain, and mood—without pressure.

Why Does Fitness Matter for Teens?

Your teen years are when:
• Your body grows the fastest
• Your brain forms habits that last
• You begin making independent choices
So the way you move, eat, rest, and enjoy now… can shape your future health.
And guess what?
AI can make healthy choices feel easier and cooler.

AI for Fitness: Your Digital Workout Buddy

Tools to Explore:

Tool	What It Does
Google Fit / Apple Health	Tracks steps, heart rate, calories
Nike Training Club / FitOn AI	Personalized workouts, challenges
Aaptiv / GymStreak / Ultrahuman	AI coaches, guided routines
Sleep Cycle / Alarmi	Smart alarms, sleep tracking
Strava	Run, cycle, walk tracking with AI maps

What AI Tracks:
• Steps & activity
• Sleep quality
• Heart rate

• Calories burned
• Goals progress

Tip: Set daily goals like "7,000 steps" or "15-min movement" Let your app cheer you on!

AI for Food & Nutrition: Eat Smart

Feeling confused by:

• What to eat before exams?
• What snacks are actually healthy?
• How to eat protein on a veg diet?

Let AI help you with:

• Meal planning
• Grocery lists
• Nutrition tracking
• Calorie counting

AI Food Tools:

Tool	What It Does
MyFitnessPal	Track meals, water, macros
Lifesum	Create smart meal plans
Yazio	Weight goals, healthy eating
HealthifyMe (India-based)	Indian meals, coaching, calorie tracking
Whisk	Suggests recipes based on fridge items
ChatGPT	**Ask:** "Suggest healthy vegetarian meals under Rs. 100."

Try This: Use HealthifyMe to scan the label of a packet snack. See how much sugar or salt it has. Shocking, right?

AI for Mindfulness & Relaxation

Your mental health matters as much as your physical health.

AI can help with:
- Meditation
- Breathing exercises
- Journaling
- Focus playlists
- Sleep stories

Chill-Out Tools:

Tool	What It Does
Headspace / Calm	Guided meditation & sleep stories
Wysa AI	Chatbot for emotional support
Insight Timer	Meditation with music
Suno / Lo-fi Generator	Create relaxing background music
Reflectly AI	Daily journaling with mood tracking

Bonus: Ask ChatGPT, "Write me a 5-minute meditation for anxiety."

AI for Fun & Music

Feeling bored or down?
Let AI create or curate joy:

Tool	What It Does
Spotify AI DJ	Personalized playlists based on mood
Suno / Udio	Create your own songs
YouTube Music AI	Suggests what you might like next
Beatleap	Add beats to your reels or videos

Boomy	Make music in minutes – no instruments needed

Challenge: Make a study anthem, a post-workout pump-up, or a bedtime lo-fi track with AI.

Try This: Your 1-Day AI Wellness Plan

Time	Task	AI Help
7:00 AM	Wake up smart	Sleep Cycle Alarm
7:30 AM	Healthy breakfast	HealthifyMe recipe
8:00 AM	15-min stretch	Nike Training Club AI
4:00 PM	Mood dip?	Calm or Suno music
7:00 PM	20-min walk	Track on Google Fit
9:00 PM	Reflect on the day	Reflectly journaling

Just try this for one day—feel the difference.

Balance Is the Key

Yes, AI helps you become healthier.
But don't let it become a pressure game.

× Don't:
- Obsess over numbers
- Compete constantly with others
- Believe every fitness influencer online

✓ Do:
- Celebrate small wins
- Use AI to discover what works for you
- Mix tech time with real-life fun

Let's Reflect

- Do you feel better after moving your body for just 10 minutes?
- What does "eating smart" mean to you?
- Could AI help you build a fun routine instead of a boring one?

Wellness & Science: What Experts Say

Research shows:

- Teens using fitness tracking apps are more active
- AI reminders help build positive habits
- Guided meditation boosts sleep and focus
- Personalized AI suggestions = longer habit stickiness

That's why schools and wellness programs now include AI-powered platforms.
Wellness is no longer about punishment.
It's about personalization—and AI helps with that.

Abeer's Tech Tip
Reset your recommendation feed occasionally. Changing your viewing patterns teaches you how algorithms adapt to behavior.
Amaara Asks
Are algorithms shaping your interests — or are your interests shaping the algorithm?

Chapter Summary

- AI can guide your physical health, meals, mood, and daily habits.
- Smartwatches, sleep apps, and fitness trackers help build better routines.
- Apps like HealthifyMe, Calm, Wysa, and Suno add fun + ease to your wellness journey.
- Use AI to stay balanced, joyful, and healthy—not pressured.

Chapter 6

AI for Time Management & Productivity

Plan Smarter, Focus Better, and Get Things Done

Let's Begin: "Too Much To Do, Too Little Time?"

You have a history test, football practice, two assignments, a birthday party, and you're already behind on your sleep.
Sound familiar?

Now imagine this:

- Your day is already planned.
- Tasks are broken down by priority.
- You get timely reminders.
- You finish work before deadlines.
- And you still have time to relax.

Sounds magical? It's not.
It's the power of AI for time management.

Why Teens Need Smart Time Tools

Teen life today = 100 tabs open in your brain.
Between school, friends, hobbies, and screen time, time feels like it's slipping away.

AI doesn't give you more time—but it helps you use time better by:

- Reducing stress
- Increasing focus
- Tracking goals
- Automating boring tasks
- Creating space for fun

The Productivity Puzzle

Time management isn't about doing everything.
It's about doing the right things at the right time.

With AI tools, you can:

- Break tasks into manageable chunks
- Schedule based on energy levels
- Set reminders you'll actually follow
- Stop procrastinating (finally!)

Let's see how.

AI Tools to Organize Your Day

Tool	What It Does	Why It's Awesome
Reclaim.ai	Auto-plans your calendar	Moves tasks around based on real life
Motion	Combines calendar + task list	Helps you focus on one thing at a time

SkedPal	Schedules smartly using your preferences	Great for ADHD brains
Notion AI	Study planner + life dashboard	All-in-one hub for teens
Trello + Butler AI	Project boards with automation	Good for group projects
Clockify / Pomofocus	Tracks how you spend time	Helps fix distractions

Bonus: Use ChatGPT to break big goals into small steps.
Ask: "Make a weekly plan to study for my board exams without burnout."

How to Use AI for Smart Scheduling

Step 1: Set Your Weekly Priorities

List your:

- Classes
- Assignments
- Study goals
- Extra activities
- Chill time

Step 2: Feed into Smart Calendar (e.g., Reclaim.ai)

- Add tasks with deadlines
- Set focus hours
- Add buffer time

Step 3: Let AI Do the Work

- It rearranges tasks
- Reminds you gently
- Helps avoid overlap or overload

Step 4: Review Every Sunday

- What worked?
- What slipped?
- Adjust for next week

Beat Procrastination with AI

AI can't stop your scrolling. But it can help you understand your habits.

Tools like:

- RescueTime – Tracks screen time and app usage
- Forest App – Grow a tree when you stay focused
- StayFree AI – Break down distractions by app
- Motion AI – Nudges you back to your plan

Tip:

If you waste 2 hours on reels, schedule "scroll time" as a reward. Don't ban fun. Balance it.

Sample Daily Routine with AI Help

Time	Activity	AI Buddy
6:45 AM	Wake up	Smart Alarm (Sleep Cycle)
7:30 AM	School prep	Reminder via Motion
4:00 PM	Homework	Study session tracked with Pomofocus
6:00 PM	Outdoor activity	Google Fit goal
7:30 PM	Revision	Notion AI flashcards
9:00 PM	Reflection	ChatGPT mood journaling

It's not about perfection. It's about making chaos manageable.

Time + Goals = Productivity

AI can also help with:
- **Goal Setting:** Use ChatGPT to draft weekly study goals
- **Habit Tracking:** Use Notion templates or Loop Habit Tracker
- **Deadlines:** Use Trello or Todoist with reminders
- **Focus Music:** Ask Suno or Spotify AI DJ to play "deep work" beats

"Try This" Productivity Challenges

Challenge 1: One-Day AI Schedule
- Use Reclaim.ai or Motion
- Let AI schedule your entire day
- Follow it and journal how you felt

Challenge 2: Pomodoro Power
- Use Pomofocus (25-min work + 5-min break)
- Do 3 rounds with a timer
- Reward yourself after

Challenge 3: Digital Detox Hour
- Schedule a "No Screen Hour"
- Use AI to suggest non-tech activities
- Reflect on your focus and mood

Let's Reflect

- What wastes most of your time each day?
- What's one thing AI could help you do quicker?
- Are you in control of your time—or just reacting?

The Mental Side of Productivity

Overworking isn't a badge of honor.

Smart productivity = Work + Rest + Joy

Use AI to:
• End overwhelm
• Track how much you've already done
• Block time for breaks

Even 15 minutes of focused work is a win.

Chapter Summary

• AI helps you manage your time through smart calendars, reminders, and planning apps.
• Use tools like Motion, Reclaim.ai, Notion, and Pomofocus to beat procrastination.
• Reflect weekly to build consistency, not perfection.
• Balance focus and fun—AI can help with both.

Chapter 7

AI for Creativity – Art, Music, Writing & Videos

Become a Digital Creator with Smart Toolsw

"Not Just a Consumer. Be a Creator."

You scroll through amazing reels.
Someone your age made a lo-fi beat with cool visuals.
Another one published a digital comic.
A classmate just posted a beautiful AI art piece.
And you wonder: Can I do this too?

The answer is: YES.

You don't need to be a professional artist, singer, or editor.
With AI, you just need ideas—and curiosity.
AI makes creativity accessible to every teen.

Why Creativity Matters

Creativity isn't just for fun. It helps you:

- Express emotions
- Solve problems
- Reduce stress
- Explore careers
- Build confidence

Whether you love drawing, rapping, journaling, editing, or storytelling—AI can help you create faster, smarter, and cooler.

AI Tools for Art & Design

Want to make:

- Digital posters?
- Insta posts?
- Abstract paintings?
- School infographics?

Here's how AI helps:

Tool	What It Does
Canva Magic	Design anything using text prompts
Midjourney	Create stunning AI images
DALL·E (OpenAI)	Turn words into pictures
Adobe Firefly	Professional-level AI design
Bing Image Creator	Free, easy AI art from text

Try This: Prompt in DALL·E: "A teen girl sitting under a neon sky with a laptop, dreaming about stars."

Boom! Instant art.

Use AI for:
- School presentations
- Digital portfolios
- Posters for events
- Memes (yes, memes!)

Bonus: Combine your photos with AI filters for extra cool effects.

AI for Writing: Stories, Poems & More

Writer's block?
AI is your co-author!

Tool	What It Does
ChatGPT	Write poems, scripts, stories
Canva Magic Write	Short form content & captions
Sudowrite	Expand, twist, or rewrite stories
Quillbot	Paraphrase & enhance text
Hemingway Editor	Make your writing bold and clear

Ideas to Try:
- "Write a poem about exams as a villain."
- "Make a short script for a funny school sketch."
- "Create a plot for a mystery story set in your city."

You can also:
- Write lyrics
- Draft blogs
- Prepare speech contests

Remember: AI gives you the seed. YOU grow the story.

AI for Music: Be Your Own DJ

Want to compose music but never learned an instrument?
No problem.

AI can help you:
- Create your own tracks
- Remix audio
- Make songs for reels or background study playlists

Tool	What It Does
Suno AI	Generate music from prompts
Udio	AI songs with lyrics & beat
Boomy	Auto-compose songs in minutes
Soundraw / Beatoven	Create music by mood
Beatleap	Match beats to your video timing

Example:
Prompt: "Make a relaxing lo-fi beat for night studying"
– Suno will give you a fully produced music clip!

AI for Videos: Become a Creator

Whether it's YouTube, school projects, or personal fun—video content stands out.

AI helps you:
- Edit fast
- Add voiceover
- Cut long videos into reels
- Add subtitles & effects

Tool	What It Does
Synthesia	Create talking avatar videos
OpusClip	Turn long videos into shorts
Runway AI	Text-to-video editing
Pictory	Turn text or blogs into videos
Descript	Edit video by editing the transcript

Example:

- Record a 1-minute explanation of a topic
- Upload to OpusClip
- Get a fun, TikTok-ready short video in 1 click!

Try This: Your AI Creativity Weekend

Pick any 2 ideas:

Goal	AI Tool
Make a song about Monday blues	Suno or Boomy
Design your dream room	Midjourney
Create a comic strip	Canva + ChatGPT
Write a poem on "Math Anxiety"	ChatGPT
Turn a paragraph into a video	Pictory
Make an Insta post for a cause	Canva Magic

Then share with friends—or just smile at what you created!

Schools & Creative Projects

Teachers love when you:

- Submit a presentation with visuals

• Use digital posters for campaigns
• Make videos for school events
• Add audio stories to language projects

You don't need expensive software—just smart AI tools and imagination.

Tip: Always give credit for AI-created art if used in competitions or formal projects.

Your Creative Portfolio Starts Now

Use Notion or Google Sites to build your own:
• Story blog
• Music collection
• Poster gallery
• Video channel

Let AI help you build something that showcases YOU.
Because being creative today is not optional—it's your superpower.

Let's Reflect

• What's something you always wanted to create?
• How can AI help you start—even if you're not "good" yet?
• How can creativity help in school and life?

Creative Ethics: Don't Just Copy-Paste

While AI helps, don't:
• Copy art and call it your own
• Use AI-generated content in contests without permission
• Rely only on prompts—put your own twist

Create with AI. Not because of it.

Abeer's Tech Tip
Use AI outputs as drafts, not final versions. Add your own voice, style, and improvements.

Amaara Asks
If AI can generate art instantly, what makes human creativity meaningful?

Chapter Summary

- AI tools can help you become a digital artist, writer, musician, or video creator—no expert skills needed.
- Use tools like Canva, Midjourney, ChatGPT, Suno, and OpusClip to express your ideas.
- Mix your imagination with AI's speed to create amazing school projects or fun content.
- Build your own portfolio and creative habits using smart apps.

Chapter 8

Virtual Assistants You Should Know

Meet the AI Buddies That Help You Think, Plan & Do More

"Hey Assistant, Can You Help?"

You're stuck on a math problem.
You forgot your to-do list.
You need to send an email but can't figure out the tone.
And you still have to revise for your exam.
You wish someone—or something—could guide you without judgment, 24/7.
Guess what? That's exactly what a virtual assistant does.
Welcome to the world of AI assistants—your digital buddies that help you talk, type, think, plan, and organize your life.

What Is a Virtual Assistant?

A virtual assistant is a smart AI program that helps you:

• Answer questions

- Organize tasks
- Solve problems
- Set reminders
- Draft emails
- Plan routines
- And even talk like a friend

They don't have a body. But they act like a digital brain—fast, friendly, and available anytime.

Think of them as your tech genie, but without the magic lamp.

Common Virtual Assistants You Already Know

Assistant	What It Does	Platforms
ChatGPT	Chat, write, explain, brainstorm	Web, App
Google Gemini	Search + Planning	Android, Web
Siri	Voice-based help	iOS
Alexa	Smart home assistant	Echo Devices
Microsoft Copilot	In Word, Excel, PowerPoint	Windows
Claude AI	Creative writing + documents	Web
Perplexity	Homework-friendly AI search	Web, App

These assistants are free or freemium, and can save hours of your time.

How They Help in Real Teen Life

Let's see how these assistants work in your routine:

Studying

- **Ask ChatGPT:** "Explain chemical bonding in easy language."
- Use Claude AI to summarize long PDF chapters.
- Use Gemini to get reliable results with links.

Planning

- **Ask ChatGPT:** "Make me a study schedule for next week with breaks."
- **Use Siri:** "Remind me to revise biology at 6 PM."
- Use Google Calendar + Gemini to schedule your exam week.

Writing

- **Ask Copilot:** "Improve my essay on climate change."
- **Use ChatGPT:** "Write a formal email to the school principal."

Creativity

- **Ask Claude:** "Write a script for a school play."
- **Use ChatGPT:** "Give me ideas for a reel about exam stress."
- Pair with Canva for designs or Pictory for videos.

Let's Compare: Which Assistant Should You Use?

Task	Best Assistant
Writing essays or stories	ChatGPT / Claude
Summarizing chapters	Claude / Gemini
Voice commands	Siri / Alexa
Scheduling & reminders	Google Gemini / Siri
Research help	Perplexity
School documents	Microsoft Copilot
Conversations	ChatGPT / Replika
Class presentations	Copilot in PowerPoint

Tip: Try each one for a week. See which fits your style best!

ChatGPT – Your All-in-One Think Buddy

Use it for:
• Definitions
• Translations
• Rewriting homework
• Generating questions
• Practicing debates
• Joke writing
• Poem creation
• Study games

Just type:
"Make a quiz of 10 MCQs from Class 10 Biology – Cell Structure"
Boom! Instant test.

Tip: The better your prompt, the better the reply.

Try being specific:
"Explain black holes in 100 words for a school science project."

Google Gemini – Smart Search + Planner

• **Ask:** "What are 5 key points from India's freedom struggle?"
• **Or:** "Summarize today's weather + add reminder for umbrella at 3 PM"
• Gemini can also plan routines and integrate with your Google apps.

It's like having Google with a brain.

Microsoft Copilot – AI in School Software

Available in Word, Excel, PowerPoint.
Use it to:
• Rephrase essays

• Add speaker notes
• Turn text into slides
• Generate charts
• Fix formatting issues

Perfect for school assignments + competitions.

Claude AI – Great for Long Answers

Claude handles long documents and deep reasoning.

Use it for:
• Reading big PDFs
• Writing thoughtful essays
• Roleplay or story building
• Project support

Ask:
"Help me create a science project outline on renewable energy."

Perplexity – For Smart Homework Research

Type a question.

It gives you:
• Quick answers
• Citations + sources
• Links to read more

Great for history, geography, or general research.

Ask: "What causes earthquakes? Give me 3 sources to read."

Try This: Assistant Battle

Pick a task—like "Summarize the chapter on photosynthesis."

Try the same prompt in:
• ChatGPT
• Claude
• Gemini
• Perplexity

Then compare:
• Which is clearer?
• Which is accurate?
• Which feels like your style?

Let's Reflect

• Have you ever wished you had a tutor on call?
• Which assistant do you trust the most—and why?
• How can these tools reduce stress, not increase it?

Be a Smart User

Don't:
• Use AI to cheat on tests
• Share personal data
• Depend on AI 100%

Do:
• Review every answer
• Learn from what it says
• Give your own twist to AI drafts

Use virtual assistants to become a real-life problem solver.

Schools & Virtual Assistants

Many NEP-aligned schools are:
• Integrating ChatGPT for creative writing
• Using Copilot for assignments
• Training students in AI literacy

You're not just a student anymore. You're a smart user in a digital world.

Chapter Summary

• Virtual assistants like ChatGPT, Gemini, Claude, Siri, and Copilot help with learning, planning, writing, and more.
• Each has strengths—use them based on your task.
• Always verify results, protect your privacy, and add your voice to AI-generated content.
• Virtual assistants = less stress, more success.

Chapter 9

Responsible AI – Staying Safe, Private & Smart

Be a Mindful, Ethical, and Safe AI User

"Just Because You Can Use AI Doesn't Mean You Should..."

You typed in a question and got a great answer.
You used AI to fix an essay.
You asked it to make jokes, generate art, or solve a math problem.
It worked. You felt smart. Efficient.

But then...

• You shared personal details in a chatbot.
• Someone in class submitted an AI-written project.
• A friend got fake news from a deepfake video.

That's where responsible AI use comes in.

This chapter isn't about scaring you.
It's about power + responsibility—the Spider-Man rule of the digital world.

Why "Responsible AI Use" Matters

AI is powerful. But it's not perfect.

It can:

- Share wrong info
- Spread bias
- Be misused for cheating or cyberbullying
- Store your private data
- Influence your decisions

You, the user, must be in control.

Rule #1: Protect Your Privacy

AI tools collect data to learn. That's not always bad—it helps them serve you better.
But you have to be careful.

Do's:

- Read the permissions an app asks for
- Use private or incognito mode when needed
- Use strong passwords
- Keep personal info (name, school, address, pictures) out of public tools
- Log out of shared devices

Don'ts:

- Don't overshare with chatbots
- Don't save passwords in AI notetaking tools
- Don't click links from unknown AI messages

Smart Teen Tip:
Always ask yourself—"Would I say this to a stranger?" If not, don't type it into AI.

Rule #2: Don't Use AI to Cheat

Let's be honest—AI can write essays, solve maths, and generate code.
It's tempting.

But remember: Shortcuts don't build skills.

Your teachers aren't checking your answers—they're building your thinking.
If AI replaces that, you lose.

Use AI to:
✓ Understand the topic
✓ Summarize and revise
✓ Draft and improve
✓ Practice quiz questions

Avoid using AI to:
× Copy-paste full homework
× Write assignments without reading
× Submit AI-written essays as your own
× Skip learning the actual subject
× Use AI as a guide—not a ghostwriter.

Rule #3: Understand That AI Can Be Wrong

AI is smart—but not all-knowing.

Sometimes it:
• Makes up facts

• Gives outdated info
• Shows cultural or gender bias
• Speaks confidently—even when wrong

Always verify:
• Dates
• Definitions
• Data
• Quotes

Cross-check with your books, teachers, or verified websites.

Rule #4: Spot AI Bias

AI is trained on human data from the internet. That means:
• It can reflect stereotypes
• It might prefer one language, gender, or culture
• It may not understand diverse perspectives

Ask:
• "Is this inclusive?"
• "Is it showing bias?"
• "What voice or point of view is missing here?"

Example:
If you ask for "a scientist," and the image is always a man—that's bias.
✓ Your job: Add your awareness. Make AI results fairer and more human.

Rule #5: Be Aware of Deepfakes & Misinformation

AI can create:
• Fake videos
• Edited voices

• AI-generated news
• False social media posts

These are called deepfakes or synthetic media.

They look real, but they're fake.

Use tools like:
• Google Reverse Image Search
• InVID browser extension
• Trusted news sites

to check the truth.

Never forward a shocking video without checking. You may be spreading lies.

Rule #6: Be Kind, Even With AI

Some people use AI to:
• Bully others with fake images
• Post rude AI-generated comments
• Send anonymous threats using bots

Don't be that person.

Use AI to:
✓ Make memes, not mockery
✓ Inspire, not insult
✓ Solve, not spread hate

Digital kindness = Real-world strength.

Try This: Responsible AI Checklist

Ask yourself before using any AI tool:
1. Am I safe? (No private data shared?)
2. Am I being honest? (No cheating or lying?)
3. Am I being kind? (No bullying or harm?)
4. Am I being mindful? (Not blindly trusting?)
5. Am I being balanced? (Not overusing tech?)

If the answer is "yes" to all → Go ahead.

Let's Reflect

• Have you ever used AI in a way that made you feel uncomfortable?
• Do you think your school needs more awareness about responsible AI use?
• What does "digital integrity" mean to you?

In Schools: Ethics + AI Education

More schools are now:
• Including AI ethics in computer science
• Discussing privacy & digital footprint
• Creating school rules for chatbot use
• Using plagiarism tools to spot AI-written homework

You can be part of that change—by being an example.

Real Life Balance: Digital Detox with AI Help

Use AI tools like:
• OneSec – Delays distracting app openings
• Focus Bear – Helps teens build habits + break phone addiction
• Daylio – Tracks mood vs screen time
• Google Wellbeing – Manages app usage

You don't have to escape tech. Just use it with awareness.

Abeer's Tech Tip
Review privacy settings on apps you use frequently. Small adjustments significantly reduce data exposure.
Amaara Asks
If convenience costs privacy, how much are we willing to trade?

Chapter Summary

- AI is powerful—but must be used responsibly.
- Protect your privacy and don't overshare.
- Never use AI to cheat or replace learning.
- Watch out for bias, misinformation, and deepfakes.
- Use AI to create value, not harm.
- Let kindness and awareness guide your digital journey.

Chapter 10

Your AI-Powered Future

Careers, Skills & Life in the Age of Intelligence

"The Future Is Closer Than You Think"

Imagine waking up in 2035.

Your smartwatch checks your health.
Your personal AI assistant updates you on world news and your college assignments.
Your career coach bot helps you practice interview questions.
And your playlist is made by—you guessed it—AI.

Now rewind.
That future? It's already taking shape—today.

Welcome to your AI-powered future—where tech, creativity, learning, and purpose collide.
Let's explore what it means for YOU.

AI Is Changing the World—Fast

Here's how AI is reshaping everything:

Area	Impact of AI
Jobs	Automating repetitive tasks, creating new tech + creative careers
Education	Personalized learning, AI tutors, smart feedback
Healthcare	Disease prediction, robotics, mental health bots
Agriculture	Smart irrigation, yield predictions, crop health alerts
Environment	Monitoring climate change, managing waste, clean energy solutions
Entertainment	AI-generated music, video editing, game design
Business	Smart marketing, virtual assistants, fraud detection

AI is not "taking over"—it's transforming the way we live and work. Your generation will not compete with AI, but collaborate with it.

What This Means for Teens

You don't need to become a data scientist (unless you want to!).

But every teen should know how to:
- Use AI tools confidently
- Think critically about AI outputs
- Communicate, create, and collaborate with tech
- Stay ethical, responsible, and mindful
- Keep learning new skills throughout life

AI will reward those who are curious, adaptive, and digitally fluent.

Future-Ready Skills to Build Now

Let's break down some future-proof skills—useful in any field:

Skill	Why It Matters in an AI World
Critical Thinking	To question AI results & make smart decisions
Creativity	To do what AI can't: imagine, innovate, inspire
Digital Literacy	To use AI tools safely and efficiently
Emotional Intelligence	To lead, collaborate, and empathize
Problem Solving	To turn AI into solutions, not just answers
Communication	To share your ideas with humans + machines
Coding Basics	Optional—but gives you superpowers!

You don't have to master everything. Start with what excites you.

Easy Ways to Start Learning AI Skills Today

You can:

- Use ChatGPT to explore topics or practice interviews
- Create with Canva, Suno, Midjourney
- Plan with Reclaim.ai or Motion
- Build apps with MIT App Inventor
- Try AI courses on Google for Teens, Khan Academy, or AI4Youth
- Join coding clubs or digital art contests
- Interview professionals using AI in your community

Real learning begins when you start creating with what you've learned.

What Kind of Careers Will Involve AI?

So many!

Here are examples from multiple fields:

Career Area	AI-Enabled Roles
Medicine	AI imaging analyst, bioinformatics expert
Art & Design	AI illustrator, interactive experience designer
Education	EdTech innovator, AI curriculum developer
Finance	Data analyst, fraud detection expert
Agriculture	Precision farming consultant
Media	Content strategist, AI video editor
Law	Legal tech consultant
Marketing	Ad targeting strategist, chatbot copywriter
Social Work	AI-for-good project manager

Even traditional careers will require digital understanding.

Jobs That May Fade (But Evolve)

AI may replace:
- Basic data entry
- Repetitive factory jobs
- Simple customer service roles
- Manual bookkeeping
- Translation (but not cultural interpretation)

But remember: New jobs will rise.
Your job is to stay flexible, creative, and ready to learn.

Plan Your Future with the "AI+Me" Formula

Step 1: Find what YOU love
Step 2: Learn how AI can support it
Step 3: Build basic digital & communication skills
Step 4: Explore internships, clubs, mentors

Step 5: Stay curious—keep updating your knowledge

Example:
Love animals? Become a vet who uses AI to detect disease in pets.
Love fashion? Use AI to design clothes based on climate data!

Future You: What Could You Be?

If You Love...	Try This
Writing	AI-aided author, blog coach, UX writer
Music	Sound designer, AI DJ
Science	Researcher using AI simulations
Environment	Climate analyst using AI sensors
Psychology	Build wellness bots
Gaming	AI game logic designer
Teaching	EdTech developer with smart feedback tools

The only limit is your creativity + values + curiosity.

Try This: "Future Me" Activity

Answer these prompts:
1. What's something I love doing?
2. How could AI make that better or easier?
3. What is one skill I want to learn this year?
4. Who in my community uses AI in their work?

Then:
• Talk to someone in that field
• Watch a YouTube video about it
• Try a mini-project using an AI tool

Start small. Stay excited. Keep growing.

Let’s Reflect

• What does your dream job look like in an AI world?
• How can you use AI as a tool, not a threat?
• What excites you most about the future?

Chapter Summary

• AI is changing how we work, live, and grow—but humans are still at the center.
• Teens who are curious, ethical, creative, and adaptive will thrive.
• Build future-ready skills: critical thinking, creativity, communication, and digital literacy.
• Explore careers across all fields—AI is everywhere.
• Your future isn't about fighting AI. It's about growing with it.

Chapter 11

Learning to Prompt Like a Pro

Master the Art of Talking to AI for Smarter Results

"You Ask. AI Answers. But Only If You Ask It Right."

Have you ever typed something into ChatGPT or another AI tool and got a weird, boring, or completely useless response?
That's not because the AI is broken.
It's because the prompt wasn't clear.
In the world of AI, your question is everything. The better your prompt, the better the result.
This chapter is all about learning how to talk to AI—like a pro.
It's like learning the language of your favorite digital helper.

What's a Prompt, Really?

A prompt is:

• A question

• A command
• A request
• Or even a roleplay setup

It's what you type or say to an AI to get a specific result.

If AI is a powerful searchlight, your prompt is the switch that turns it on and aims it right.

Anatomy of a Great Prompt

Here's what a good prompt usually includes:

Element	What It Does	Example
Instruction	Tells AI what to do	"Summarize this text..."
Context	Gives background info	"I'm a Class 10 student..."
Tone/Format	Sets style or structure	"Write it like a funny poem."
Constraints	Adds limits or rules	"Keep it under 100 words."
Persona/Role	Makes AI act like someone	"Act like my history teacher..."

Just like giving directions to a friend—be clear, specific, and polite.

Prompt Examples: Before vs. After

× Weak Prompt:
"Explain climate change."

✓ Strong Prompt:

"Explain climate change to a 14-year-old student in simple language, using a cricket match analogy. Keep it under 150 words."

Result: Way better, clearer, more fun!

× Weak Prompt:
"Make a schedule."

✓ Strong Prompt:
"Create a weekly study schedule for a Class 12 student with 6 subjects, 4 hours daily, including revision and breaks. Make it in table format."

Now the AI knows exactly what to do.

Prompt Templates for Teens

Study
"Summarize this [paste topic] in bullet points for exam revision."
"Make a 5-question quiz on [topic] with answers."
"Explain [topic] like I'm 10 years old."

Writing
"Rewrite this paragraph to sound more confident and formal."
"Turn this into a speech for school assembly."
"Write a story with a plot twist about a student who finds a secret AI app."

Creativity
"Write a rap about exam stress in the style of a stand-up comedian."
"Give me 10 content ideas for an Instagram account about books and study tips."
"Describe a dream room that combines tech and tradition. I want to draw it."

Communication
"Write a respectful message to my teacher asking for an extension."
"Draft an apology text to a friend after an argument, with empathy."
"Give me 3 subject lines for an email asking for a school letter."

Prompt Challenges: Let's Practice!

Try improving these basic prompts:
1. **Bad Prompt:** "Tell me about AI."
Better Prompt: "Give me a teen-friendly definition of Artificial Intelligence, with an example from everyday life."
2. **Bad Prompt**: "Write a poem."
Better Prompt: "Write a 4-line funny poem about why students hate Monday mornings."
3. **Bad Prompt**: "Make a project."
Better Prompt: "Create a Class 11 biology project outline on 'Human Circulatory System' with 3 sections, one visual, and one fun fact."

Prompt Stacking – Going Deeper

Sometimes, you won't get the perfect answer the first time. No worries.

Use prompt stacking:
Step 1: Ask the AI something basic
→ "Explain the digestive system."

Step 2: Go deeper
→ "Now add a comic-style explanation with emojis."
→ "Summarize it into a one-minute speech for a science fair."
→ "Add 3 MCQs with answers."

The more you build on it, the better your result gets.

Roles You Can Ask AI to Play

Try:
• "Act like a career counselor."
• "Pretend to be a TED speaker."
• "Be my time management coach."
• "Play the role of my debate opponent."
• "Act like a friend giving honest advice."

It's like choosing your own teacher, guide, or buddy—on demand.

Let's Reflect

• Do you just "type and hope"—or do you guide the AI?
• What was your best prompt so far? Why did it work?
• What would help you prompt better—more patience or more structure?

✓ Prompt Safety Rules

Even when prompting, always:
• Avoid sharing private details
• Don't ask harmful or inappropriate questions
• Check facts if using AI for school work
• Add your own edits—don't submit raw AI work
You're the creator. AI is your co-writer.

Real-Life Applications: Why Prompting = Power

• School projects = Faster & better
• Social media = Catchy & clever
• Daily tasks = Organized & smooth
• Career prep = Interview + CV help
• Personal growth = Journaling, affirmations, planning
Learning how to prompt = becoming tech fluent and future-ready.

Prompt Pack: Save These!

Task	Prompt
Essay help	"Improve my essay on water scarcity. Make it more impactful, under 300 words."
Content idea	"Give 10 video ideas about smart studying for a teen creator."
Wellness	"Create a 7-day digital detox plan for a student with exam stress."
Revision	"Explain democracy using an Indian classroom example."
Career	"List 5 AI-based careers that combine science and creativity."

Chapter Summary

- A prompt is how you "talk" to AI—it must be clear, specific, and well-structured.
- Use prompt elements: instruction, tone, context, constraints, and role.
- Practice turning vague prompts into better ones.
- Explore different prompt styles—quizzes, stories, captions, conversations.
- Great prompting = smarter outputs = time saved + quality boosted.

Chapter 12

Smart Parenting with AI

How Teens Can Help Their Families Use Technology Wisely

"Beta, Ye ChatGPT Kya Hota Hai?"

If you've ever:
• Helped your mom figure out WhatsApp storage,
• Set up Alexa for your grandparents,
• Explained YouTube privacy settings to your dad,
—then you've already taken your first step as a Teen Tech Guide.

In this chapter, you'll discover how YOU can help your family use

AI tools for:
• Daily life
• Safety
• Health
• Shopping
• And building trust in technology

AI isn't just for school and social media.
It can also make family life smarter—and you can lead the way.

Why This Matters

Most parents didn't grow up with AI.
They may feel confused, scared, or even mistrustful of it.

Your role is to:

- Bridge the digital gap
- Introduce tech in simple ways
- Protect your family from tech misuse
- Empower everyone—without judging

You don't need to "teach" like a boss.
Just guide with patience, kindness, and small steps.

AI at Home: Use Cases That Make Life Easier

1. Voice Assistants

Task	Tool	Use
"Alexa, play Hanuman Chalisa"	Alexa / Google Assistant	Voice commands for music, prayers
"Remind me to take BP medicine at 9 AM"	Siri / Google Assistant	Medication alerts
"What's the weather in Varanasi?"	Gemini / Alexa	Weather updates in local language

Help family members speak to AI rather than type.

2. Shopping & Household Management

Task	Tool	Use
Weekly grocery planner	ChatGPT	Ask: "Make a 7-day vegetarian meal plan with a shopping list."
Budget tracking	Copilot in Excel	Smart calculations of monthly bills
Online comparisons	Perplexity / Gemini	"Compare refriger-ator under 25,000 with reviews."

Tip: Create a shared Google Sheet with your family to track spending.

3. Recipes & Kitchen Time

Task	Tool	Use
AI meal planncr	HealthifyMe, ChatGPT	Get healthy ideas based on fridge items
Waste-less cooking	Whisk	Recipe ideas using leftover food
Audio instructions	YouTube + Alexa	Listen to step-by-step recipes while cooking

Show your parents how to search recipes using specific ingredients.

4. Learning & Language

Task	Tool	Use
Translate English to Hindi	Google Translate	Help parents read forms, menus, medicine labels
Voice typing	Gboard	Teach elders to speak instead of type
Explain tech news	ChatGPT	Ask: "Explain the UPI payment system in simple Hindi."

Ask AI to explain tricky topics to your parents in your regional language.

5. Safety & Awareness

Task	Tool	Use
Block scammy sites	Safe Browsing tools	Enable safety filters in browsers
Recognize deepfakes	InVID plugin	Show how fake news spreads via AI
Privacy protection	Device settings	Help set app permissions + strong passwords

Empower elders to ask: "Is this real?" before sharing anything online.

Conversation Starters with Parents

- "Did you know we can use AI to plan our grocery budget?"
- "Want me to show you how to use voice commands on your phone?"

• "Let's create a reminder for your doctor's visit together."
• "Can I show you how to check news using Gemini or YouTube Shorts in Hindi?"
• "You don't have to be 'tech-savvy.' Just curious is enough."

Family Projects You Can Do with AI

Project	Tools	Goal
Family Recipe Book	ChatGPT + Canva	Ask AI to organize family recipes into a printable booklet
Monthly Health Planner	Google Sheets + Notion	Track steps, water intake, appointments
Travel Itinerary	ChatGPT + Google Maps	Ask: "Plan a 2-day family trip to Jaipur with budget tips."
Photo Album Captions	Canva AI	Create captions, print quotes for albums
Daily Affirmation Wall	ChatGPT + Print	Ask AI to generate 30 positive quotes in Hindi/English

AI can be used to connect generations, not replace them.

Try This: The "Parent Buddy" Challenge

Pick any adult in your home—mom, dad, nani, chachu—and do this:

1. **Ask:** "What is one daily task that feels difficult for you?"
2. Suggest an AI tool that can help
3. Set it up together
4. Let them try it for 3 days
5. **Ask:** "How did it feel?"

You just became a home tech coach—without even realizing it.

Common Fears Parents Have About AI

Fear	Your Response
"AI will take jobs!"	"It may change jobs—but new skills and roles will appear too."
"It's unsafe or manipulative."	"Yes, if misused. But we can set boundaries and privacy settings."
"It's too complicated for me."	"Let's try one small thing—like using voice search."
"What if I make a mistake?"	"There's no exam here—just trial and fun."

Let's Reflect

- Who in your home could benefit most from AI?
- How can you introduce tools slowly and respectfully?
- How can families grow together with AI?

Real-Life Story: Ayush (Age 16, Lucknow)

Ayush taught his grandmother how to use Google Assistant to listen to Ramayana podcasts.
Now, she asks her phone to play bhajans and jokes—and even reminds him of his homework time.
"It brought us closer. Now she thinks I'm a genius!" – Ayush

Chapter Summary

- You can help your family use AI for health, groceries, learning, and memories.
- Focus on voice tools, language translation, and everyday planning.
- Be patient, respectful, and celebrate small tech wins together.
- Use AI to make home life easier, not harder.
- Smart parenting begins with smart teen helping.

Chapter 13

AI in Indian Classrooms

From NEP 2020 to AI4Youth: How Schools Are Evolving

"From Blackboards to Smart Boards—And Now AI!"

Imagine this:
Your class begins with a smart board that adapts to your pace.

Your teacher uses AI to prepare quizzes based on your performance.
Your homework is reviewed by an app that gives instant feedback.
Your classroom has a voice assistant that helps answer your questions.

This is not the future.
This is already happening in some schools—and soon, it could be yours too.
In this chapter, you'll explore how India's education system is embracing AI—and how you are a part of it.

NEP 2020: What It Says About Tech & AI

India's National Education Policy 2020 (NEP 2020) encourages:

- Digital tools for learning
- AI integration across school subjects
- Tech-based assessments
- Personalized learning
- Skill-building for 21st-century careers

"Students must not just use technology—they must learn to understand, create, and use it mindfully."
AI isn't an "extra subject"—it's a life skill.

What is "AI Literacy"?

AI literacy means:

- Knowing what AI is
- Understanding how it works
- Using AI tools smartly
- Thinking critically about AI
- Knowing where and how to apply it

You don't have to be a coder or data scientist.
You just need to be digitally aware, safe, and curious.

How AI Is Already in Schools

Area	How AI Is Used
Teaching	Teachers use AI to plan lessons, check homework, and create personalized quizzes
Smart Boards	Interactive digital boards respond to students' pace and learning levels
Assessment	AI apps help in grading essays and detecting plagiarism

Learning Tools	Platforms like Diksha, BYJU'S, Toppr use AI to adapt lessons
Career Guidance	Tools suggest career options based on your interests and strengths
Language Learning	Translation, pronunciation, and speech tools help students in regional areas

Programs You Should Know

1. AI4Youth (CBSE + Intel)

• Launched for Classes 8–12
• Hands-on AI training
• Focuses on AI ethics, creativity, and problem-solving
• Offers toolkits, workshops, and project mentorship
• Available in CBSE schools nationwide

2. ATL Tinkering Labs (NITI Aayog)

• Set up in thousands of schools
• Focus on coding, AI, and innovation
• Robotics, sensors, AI-based games and projects
• Encourages girls and rural students to join tech missions

3. IndiaAI Mission (MeitY)

• National initiative to build AI skills
• Partnerships with schools, colleges, and youth clubs
• Free online resources for students

Real School Examples

• **Amity International School, Noida:** AI-powered science projects using Python and machine learning.
• **Kendriya Vidyalayas:** Participating in CBSE AI4Youth, students developed chatbots for school library help.
• **Rural schools in Kerala:** Using voice-based AI in Malayalam for

math practice.
Tech doesn't depend on money. It depends on mindset.

What Students Are Creating

Student	Project	AI Used
Anika (Class 10)	Mental health bot for teens	NLP + ChatGPT
Rohan (Class 9)	Flood prediction model	Python + data visualization
Sara (Class 11)	Smart timetable planner	Notion + Reclaim
Team @ School Club	Plastic waste classifier app	Image recognition

If they can, so can you.

School Project Ideas with AI

Here are AI-powered ideas you can suggest in class:

Subject	Project Idea
English	Create AI-generated poetry and analyze tone changes
Science	Use AI to simulate climate change scenarios
Math	Build an AI bot to quiz classmates
History	Make an AI-based virtual museum tour
Art	Use Midjourney to recreate Mughal architecture
Sanskrit/Hindi	Translate verses using Google Translate AI, then refine manually

Tip: Use Canva + ChatGPT + Pictory to create beautiful school presentations.

Tools for Indian Classrooms

Tool	Use
ChatGPT	Notes, Q&A, summaries
Google Gemini	Quick research, reminders
Pictory	Turn lessons into videos
Canva AI	Posters, charts, presentations
Microsoft Copilot	Slide creation, formatting
AI Doodle Tools	Create learning illustrations
Suno / Udio	Generate songs for learning rhymes, facts

Let's Reflect

- Does your school use smart boards or AI apps?
- What's one way your class can benefit from AI tools?
- Would you want an AI Club in your school?

Start an AI Club in Your School

Step 1: Talk to a teacher you trust
Step 2: Gather 5–10 interested students
Step 3: Pick a monthly theme (AI in art, AI in social impact)
Step 4: Use free tools and explore projects
Step 5: Host mini challenges or exhibitions
Need help? Use ChatGPT to plan club sessions!

Safety in Classrooms

Always:

- Use school-approved tools
- Don't share personal data on public AI platforms

• Don't use AI to cheat—use it to learn
• Keep balance: AI is a tool, not a teacher replacement

Real Story: Ayushi, Class 11, Ahmedabad

"I used ChatGPT to write questions for our biology quiz. Then we used Canva to make a cool visual quiz deck. Our teacher was so impressed—we now use it every week!"

Chapter Summary

• NEP 2020 encourages using AI for skill-building, learning, and creativity
• Programs like AI4Youth, ATL Labs, and IndiaAI are empowering students
• AI is helping in assessments, learning, and student-led innovation
• You can use AI for school projects, clubs, and career prep—safely and smartly
• Your classroom can be your launchpad for AI success

Chapter 14

Tech for Good

Teen Changemakers Using AI to Solve Real-World Problems

"Can Teenagers Change the World with AI?"

The answer is: Yes. Absolutely.
You don't need a tech degree.
You don't need to live in Silicon Valley.

You need just three things:
• A problem you care about
• A basic understanding of AI
• A desire to make life better for someone
This chapter is about teen heroes using AI for real-world impact—from climate change to mental health—and how you can do it too.

What Is "Tech for Good"?

"Tech for Good" means using technology—especially AI—

• Not just to earn money
• Not just to automate tasks
• But to solve social, environmental, and emotional challenges

It's compassion-powered coding.
It's human-centered innovation.

If AI is smart, then you must be wise in how you use it.

Real Stories of Teen Changemakers

1. Arjun (Age 17, Hyderabad)
Built an AI chatbot to answer COVID-19 vaccine queries in Telugu
Used: ChatGPT API + voice assistant + Google Translate
Impact: Helped elders in his area book vaccines and understand side effects

2. Maya & Simran (Age 16, Delhi)
Created a plastic sorting app using image recognition
Used: Teachable Machine + React App
Impact: Deployed in their school canteen to sort biodegradable vs plastic

3. Aditya (Age 15, Pune)
Built a mood tracker bot for teens with anxiety
Used: Google Sheets + AI plugin + Telegram Bot
Impact: Over 500 students use it for mental wellness support

4. Tanya (Age 17, Jodhpur)
Developed a Hindi-English reading assistant for Class 4 kids
Used: Whisper API + Canva + PPT voice overlay
Impact: Used in her mother's government school for reading classes

Ideas for AI Social Impact Projects (That You Can Start)

Area	Problem	AI Project Idea
Environment	Littering in parks	Image-based waste detection app
Mental Health	Teens feel lonely	AI-powered journal that gives positive affirmations
Health	Medicine reminders for elders	Voice assistant setup + AI calendar
Education	Girls dropping out	WhatsApp chatbot that shares scholarship info
Accessibility	Hearing-impaired students	Use AI to generate subtitles from audio

You don't need a lab. Just a laptop, curiosity, and courage.

AI Tools You Can Use for Good

Tool	Use	Social Impact Use Case
Teachable Machine (Google)	No-code AI model	Classify plastic vs paper waste
ChatGPT	Writing + Q&A	Create awareness posters in any language
Suno / Udio	Music generator	Compose mental health campaign jingles
Canva AI	Visual tools	Design flyers, infographics, event invites

Pictory / Veed.io	Video AI	Create explainer videos for rural kids
Whisper API	Speech-to-text	Create subtitles for health awareness videos

Mini Challenge: "Solve with AI"

1. Choose a problem you care about
2. Ask: Can AI help reduce this problem?
3. Use free tools to prototype an idea
4. Share it with friends, teachers, or a local NGO
5. Collect feedback and keep improving

Hint: Use ChatGPT to brainstorm ideas and tools step-by-step.

Join AI Youth Movements in India

AI For Youth (CBSE x Intel)
- Be part of national-level innovation challenges
- Learn AI ethics, tools, and deploy real-world projects
- Win prizes, recognition, and mentorship

Young Tinker Innovators Program (NITI Aayog)
- Build your innovation profile with support
- AI + robotics + environment + social change

UN SDGs + AI Clubs

- **Align your AI project with Sustainable Development Goals like:**
    - o Quality Education (Goal 4)
    - o Climate Action (Goal 13)
    - o Gender Equality (Goal 5)

Ethics: Tech for Good = Good with Tech

Tech for Good requires:
• Not just technical skill—but ethical wisdom
• Asking "Should I?" not just "Can I?"

For example:
• Don't track people without consent
• Don't automate something that harms livelihoods
• Always test for bias, respect privacy, and stay inclusive

Use AI as a force for empathy, not exploitation.

Let's Reflect

• What is one problem around you that really bothers you?
• Could AI help reduce or solve that problem?
• Who can you partner with to make your idea real?

You don't need to be a genius.
You need to care deeply and act smartly.

School Activity Idea: "Hack for Humanity – 1-Day AI-a-thon"

Time: 5–6 hours
Teams of 3–4 students
Goal: Solve a school/community problem using AI
Tools: Canva AI, ChatGPT, Teachable Machine, Suno
Prize: Certificate + showcase in morning assembly!

Real Story: Kabir & Team, Age 16, Ranchi

Kabir and his friends built a chatbot that helped farmers understand weather forecasts in local dialects. They partnered with their school's

IT teacher and shared it at a local mela.

"We used AI—but the real skill was teamwork and empathy," said Kabir.

Chapter Summary

- Tech for Good = Using AI to solve real problems
- Many Indian teens are already making change with AI
- You can build mood trackers, sorting apps, audio guides, and bots
- Free tools are enough—start small, grow with feedback
- Align your projects with school, community, and SDGs

Chapter 15

The Future of You

Careers, Life Skills & AI in the World Ahead

"What Will You Be When You Grow Up – In the AI Age?"

Doctor? Engineer? Artist? Data Scientist?
What if your future job doesn't exist yet?

With AI evolving so fast, the future isn't just about choosing a job. It's about learning how to learn, adapt, and create in a smart, tech-powered world.

This chapter is your guide to understanding:

- What jobs AI will impact
- What careers AI will create
- What life skills you need to thrive
- And how to prepare now

AI Is Not Taking Jobs. It's Changing Jobs.

AI won't "steal" all jobs—but it will:
• Automate repetitive tasks
• Assist decision-making
• Change how we work in every field

The future needs human + AI collaboration.

Think:
Human: Empathy, Creativity, Judgement
AI: Speed, Pattern Recognition, Repetition

Together = Superhuman performance

Jobs AI Is Transforming

Field	Traditional Role	AI-Enhanced Role
Medicine	Radiologist	AI-assisted diagnosis expert
Journalism	Reporter	AI + data storytelling editor
Education	Teacher	Tech-integrated learning guide
Law	Paralegal	AI document analyzer
Agriculture	Farmer	Smart farming analyst
Retail	Cashier	Digital sales advisor
Customer Service	Call rep	Chatbot + human hybrid role

Even artists, musicians, and fashion designers are using AI now!

Emerging Careers You Can Explore

Career Path	What It Involves
AI Prompt Engineer	Writing creative, effective prompts for AI tools
Data Analyst	Studying patterns in data with AI support
AI Ethics Officer	Ensuring tech is fair, safe, and inclusive
Digital Product Designer	Creating apps powered by AI
AI Trainer	Teaching AI models how to think better
Voice App Developer	Creating Alexa/Google Assistant skills
Virtual World Builder	Designing metaverse spaces with AI tools

You can start learning these right now with free resources!

Future-Ready Life Skills to Learn Today

Even if you don't want a tech job, you still need these 5 super skills:

1. Problem Solving
– Think logically. Break problems into steps.

Try: Solving real problems with ChatGPT, puzzle games, project-based learning.

2. Digital Literacy
– Understand how apps, AI, and data work.

Try: Use different AI tools (design, audio, planner) weekly.

3. Communication
– Speak, write, and present clearly (even with AI help!).

Try: Use Grammarly, Canva AI, ChatGPT to improve tone and clarity.

4. Ethical Thinking
– **Ask:** Is this fair? Is it biased? Is it safe?

Try: Discuss AI news with friends or join school AI clubs.

5. Adaptability & Curiosity
The future changes fast. Be ready to learn anything.

Try: Pick one new tool to learn every month.

Courses & Platforms to Learn Future Skills

Platform	Focus	Teen-Friendly Option
CBSE AI Curriculum	AI basics	Class 9–12 modules
AI4Youth (Intel India)	Hands-on AI projects	Free toolkits for students
Harvard CS50x AI	Introduction to AI coding	For advanced learners
Code.org AI Lab	Beginner AI games	Ages 13+
Khan Academy	Computer science	Teen-aligned explanations
SkillUp (Simplilearn)	Data/AI fundamentals	Career starter programs

Bonus: Learn storytelling + Canva + ChatGPT = Ultimate future combo!

AI + YOU = Unique Career Mix

You can blend AI with your passion. Here's how:

Your Interest	AI-Enhanced Career
Drawing	AI concept artist (Midjourney, DALL·E)
Music	AI music composer (Suno, Udio)
Teaching	EdTech content creator (ChatGPT + Canva)
Psychology	AI mental health tool developer
Business	Digital startup founder (AI-powered idea)
Languages	AI translation app tester, NLP editor
History	Interactive virtual museum designer

Your creativity is the secret ingredient AI will never replace.

How to Prepare in School

- Join your school's AI or Coding Club
- Organize a Tech for Good Fair
- Create a portfolio of AI-based school projects
- Take free courses during vacations
- Talk to mentors or seniors using AI in careers

Save your projects, prompts, and learnings—they'll be your future resume.

Let's Reflect

• What's your dream career? Can AI help you reach it faster?
• Are you learning life skills that can't be automated?
• What small step can you take today to prepare for tomorrow?
Don't just prepare for the future—participate in creating it.

Real Story: Zoya, Class 12, Lucknow

Zoya wanted to become a fashion designer. She began using Midjourney to generate design ideas and Canva AI to create client portfolios.
Now, she's working on a personal brand even before entering college.

"AI gave me a head start. I still do the sketching—but smarter, faster, and with confidence."

Abeer's Tech Tip
Build skills that AI complements — communication, problem-solving, empathy. These remain uniquely human strengths.
Amaara Asks
Will the future reward speed and automation — or wisdom and judgment?

Chapter Summary

• AI will change every job—but not replace human creativity, empathy, and curiosity
• Future careers need a mix of tech + human skills
• Learn problem solving, communication, adaptability, and ethical tech use
• Use AI tools to amplify your strengths and build your unique future path
• Start now: explore, experiment, and evolve

Glossary

A quick reference to understand key AI terms introduced in the book—especially useful for revision and confidence building.

Glossary – Speak AI Like a Pro

Term	Definition (Teen-Friendly)
AI (Artificial Intelligence)	Smart computer programs that can think, learn, and solve problems like humans.
Machine Learning	A way for AI to learn from data and improve over time without being told exactly what to do.
Chatbot	An AI tool that talks to you using text or voice—like ChatGPT, Siri, or Alexa.
Virtual Assistant	A digital helper that performs tasks like scheduling, searching, or writing—e.g., Google Gemini, Copilot.
Prompt	The question or instruction you give an AI tool to get a helpful response.
Algorithm	A set of instructions the AI follows to make decisions. Like a recipe for the computer!
Bias (in AI)	When AI gives unfair results due to patterns in the data it's trained on—like showing only one kind of person in search results.
Deepfake	Fake images, audio, or videos made by AI to look and sound real, but they're not!

Personalization	When AI changes what it shows you based on your behavior, like Netflix suggestions.
Digital Literacy	Knowing how to use technology (like AI) safely, smartly, and responsibly.
Text-to-Image AI	A tool that turns written descriptions into pictures. Examples: DALL·E, Midjourney.
Text-to-Speech AI	AI that reads out text in a human-like voice—used in language tools and audio-books.
Productivity App	Tools like Motion or Reclaim that use AI to help you plan, organize, and track work.
Creative AI	AI used for writing, art, music, and video creation.
Ethical AI Use	Using AI in a way that's honest, kind, and fair to others—and doesn't cause harm.
Plagiarism	Copying someone else's work—including AI's—without giving credit.
Digital Footprint	The trail of data you leave when you use apps, websites, and online tools.
Coding / Programming	Writing instructions that computers fol-low—useful but not required to use AI.
Smart Scheduling	AI that helps you plan your day by auto-matically adding tasks based on your time.
AI Agent	A small AI system that works independent-ly—like your smartwatch that reminds you to drink water.

Bonus Section: AI Tools Directory for Teens

Smart Tools for Study, Creation, Wellness & More

Each tool below is selected to support productivity, creativity, and well-being for teenagers in Grades 9–12. (Most are free or freemium!)

Productivity & Time Management

Tool	Purpose	Use Case	Link
Reclaim.ai	Smart calendar planner	Auto-schedules tasks and meetings	reclaim.ai
Motion	Calendar + task manager	Plans your week based on deadlines	usemotion.com
SkedPal	Adaptive scheduling	Plans based on habits & preferences	skedpal.com
Clockify / Pomofocus	Time tracking	Focus sessions, breaks, study timers	pomofocus.io
Notion AI	All-in-one dashboard	Plan study, track goals, write notes	notion.so/ai

Study & Writing Helpers

Tool	Purpose	Use Case	Link
ChatGPT	Q&A, content help	Essays, summaries, concept explanation	chat.openai.com
Claude AI	Long document understanding	Read/interpret PDFs and write smart content	claude.ai
Grammarly	Writing feedback	Correct grammar, tone, and clarity	grammarly.com
Quillbot	Paraphrasing	Rewriting and improving sentences	quillbot.com
PDFgear	PDF reader with AI	Summarize textbooks and notes	pdfgear.com
Perplexity AI	Smart search	Research with citations	perplexity.ai
Google Gemini	Search + planning agent	Get summaries, facts, answers	gemini.google.com

Art, Design & Posters

Tool	Purpose	Use Case	Link
Canva Magic Design	Posters, social graphics	School projects, Insta content	canva.com
Midjourney	AI-generated art	Abstract, futuristic, fantasy images	midjourney.com
DALL·E 3	Text-to-image AI	Turn prompts into realistic images	openai.com/dall-e
Adobe Firefly	Pro-level AI art	Branding, content creation	firefly.adobe.com

Video & Storytelling Tools

Tool	Purpose	Use Case	Link
OpusClip	Video clipping	Turn long videos into shorts	opus.pro
Pictory	Text-to-video	Turn blogs/scripts into videos	pictory.ai
Synthesia	Talking avatars	AI presenter for school explainer videos	synthesia.io
Descript	Transcript video editing	Edit videos by editing the text	descript.com
Runway AI	Video enhancement	AI-powered editing tools	runwayml.com

Audio, Music & Podcast Tools

Tool	Purpose	Use Case	Link
Suno AI	Music generation	Compose lo-fi beats, songs	suno.ai
Boomy	Instant music creation	Make tracks without instruments	boomy.com
Murf / ElevenLabs	Voice-over AI	Narration for projects/videos	elevenlabs.io
Beatleap	Music for videos	Edit beat-based reels & stories	beatleap.app

Wellness & Mental Health

Tool	Purpose	Use Case	Link
Wysa AI	Emotional support chatbot	Journaling, anxiety conversations	wysa.io
Reflectly	Mood tracker journal	Daily reflection & habit tracking	reflectly.app
Headspace / Calm	Meditation, sleep aid	Focus, breathing, bedtime stories	headspace.com
Focus Bear / OneSec	Distraction control	Delay app openings, build habits	focusbear.io
Sleep Cycle	Sleep tracker + smart alarm	Improve rest, track energy	sleepcycle.com

Smart Assistants & Chatbots

Tool	Purpose	Use Case	Link
Google Gemini	Info + planner	Ask questions, schedule tasks	gemini.google.com
ChatGPT	General assistant	Write, plan, explain	chat.openai.com
Claude AI	Long input expert	PDFs, deep Q&A, reports	claude.ai
Siri / Alexa / Google Assistant	Voice help	Smart commands, reminders	Device-based
Microsoft Copilot	In Office apps	Writing, formatting, slides	microsoft.com

Digital Safety & Detox Tools

Tool	Purpose	Use Case	Link
Google Family Link	Screen time & safety	Parental controls & app time limits	families.google.com
Digital Wellbeing (Android)	Usage dashboard	Track screen time, app limits	On Android devices
StayFree	Distraction tracking	See how time is spent	stayfree.me
OneSec App	Delay opening social apps	Pause → Reflect → Enter	onesec.app

Tip for Teens: Bookmark this directory. Pick 1–2 tools from each

category to try this month.
Soon, you'll discover your personalized "AI Stack" that supports your life, learning, and growth.

Summary: What You've Learned (And Why It Matters)

Artificial Intelligence is not just a future idea—it's part of your life right now. From the alarm that wakes you up to the chatbot that helps you revise for a test, AI is quietly working behind the scenes to make your day smarter, easier, and more fun.

This book helped you explore how to:

- Understand AI in simple words
- Spot AI in your home, phone, and school
- Use AI tools to study better and organize your time
- Create music, art, videos, and stories with AI
- Talk and communicate more clearly with AI help
- Stay safe, kind, and responsible while using smart tech
- Explore future-ready careers and skills in an AI-powered world

Chapter Quick Recap

Chapter	Key Takeaway
1. What is AI, Really?	AI is smart software that learns from data and helps you with everyday tasks.
2. AI Agents All Around You	Your fridge, phone, and apps are filled with AI agents helping you silently.
3. Using AI to Study Smarter	Use tools like Notion, ChatGPT, and Quizlet to make learning easier.

4. AI for Communication & Social Life	AI can help write emails, captions, and even improve how you express yourself.
5. Fitness, Food & Fun – The AI Way	Smart apps can guide your wellness, workouts, nutrition, and mental health.
6. AI for Time Management & Productivity	Plan, schedule, and focus better with AI assistants like Reclaim and Motion.
7. AI for Creativity – Art, Music, Writing & Videos	Create like a pro using tools like Midjourney, Canva, Suno, and more.
8. Virtual Assistants You Should Know	Meet digital helpers like ChatGPT, Gemini, Siri, and Copilot that guide your day.
9. Responsible AI – Staying Safe, Private & Smart	Use AI wisely—protect your data, think critically, and be ethical.
10. Your AI-Powered Future	Build future-ready skills. Learn to use AI as a tool—not a threat—to create your own path.

Final Message to You

Dear reader,

This book was created to help you not just use AI, but use it wisely—to grow, to create, to organize, and to imagine your future. You don't need to become a computer genius to thrive in an AI world.

You just need to stay:
- Curious
- Ethical
- Confident
- Creative

Always ask:
"How can this tool help me become better—not just faster?"

And remember:
The smartest tech is still YOU. AI is here to assist—but you are the one who decides what kind of world to build.

So go ahead.
Live smart.
Think kind.
Create boldly.
Use AI to become the best version of yourself.